The Joy of Russian Piano Music

A graded collection of melodic masterpieces from the romantic and modern repertory. Selected and edited by Denes Agay.

"Romanticism" is the style-signature of this volume, containing 39 works by Russian composers of the 19th and 20th centuries. In addition to their romantic pre-disposition, most of these writers are also influenced and inspired by strong nationalistic trends and undercurrents which render their music even more vivid and attractive.

The selections are all in their original forms and fall well within the easy-to-intermediate grade levels. As a whole this collection provides teacher, pupil, and player of any age not only with interesting and useful study materials, but also musical enjoyment of a high order.

Denes Agay

Order No YK 21285
US International Standard Book Number 978 0825 68032 8
UK International Standard Book Number 0 7119 0524 X

EXCLUSIVELY DISTRIBUTED BY

HAL•LEONARD®

Contents

Cradle Song

from Op. 24

Mikhael Iordansky

Gently moving

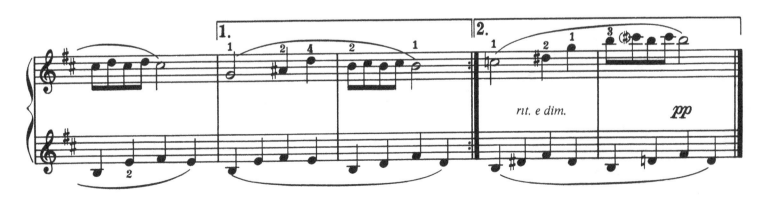

Little Tune with Variations

Leo Lukomsky

Var. III

Invention

Sergei Liapunov
(1859 - 1924)

A Little Fairy-Tale
Op. 27, No. 5

Dmitri Kabalevsky
(1904 -   )

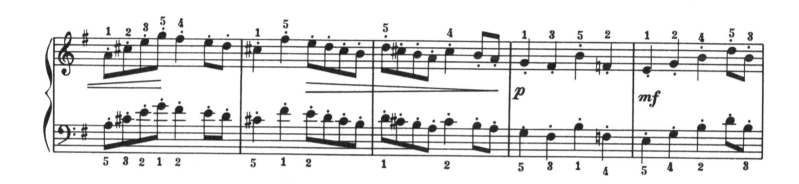

Polka

Mikhail Glinka
(1804 - 1857)

Barcarolle

Alexander Goedicke

Whistling Sailors

Samuel Maykapar
(1867 - 1938)

An Old Ballad
from Op. 24

Mikhael Iordansky

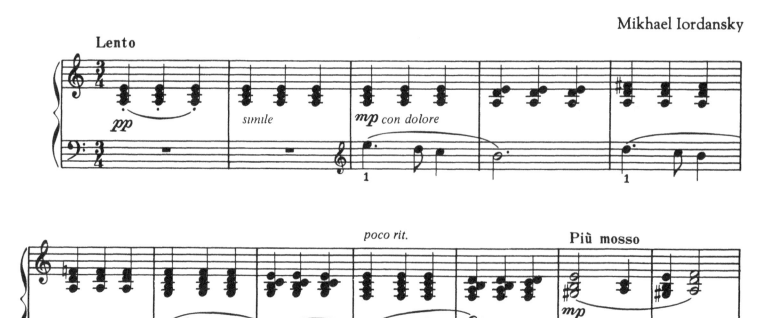

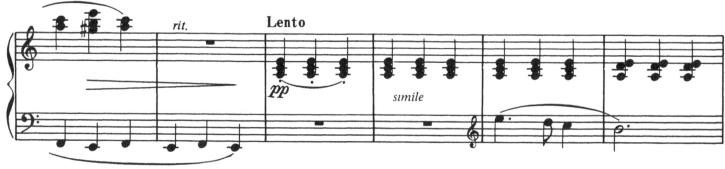

Folk Tune Scherzo

Op. 4, No. 14

Konstantin Sorokin

Shepherd Playing His Pipe

Op. 31, No. 8

Vladimir Rebikov
(1866 - 1920)

Valsette

for Natalie

Peter I. Tchaikovsky
(1840 - 1893)

*Lower notes of octaves may be omitted.

Mazurka

Mikhail Glinka
(1804 - 1857)

Dedicated to the composer's wife.

The Mechanical Doll

from Six Children's Pieces

Dmitri Shostakovich
(1906 - 1975)

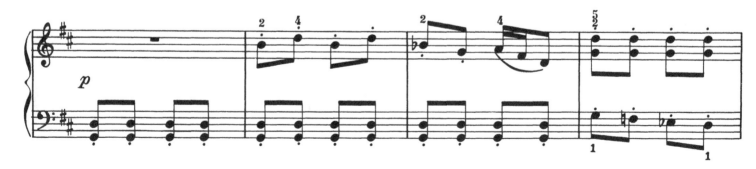

Moderato
from The Five Fingers

Igor Stravinsky
(1882 - 1971)

Lento
from The Five Fingers

Igor Stravinsky
(1882 - 1971)

Sonatina

Alexander Glazunov
(1865 - 1936)

Andante con espressione

Allegretto

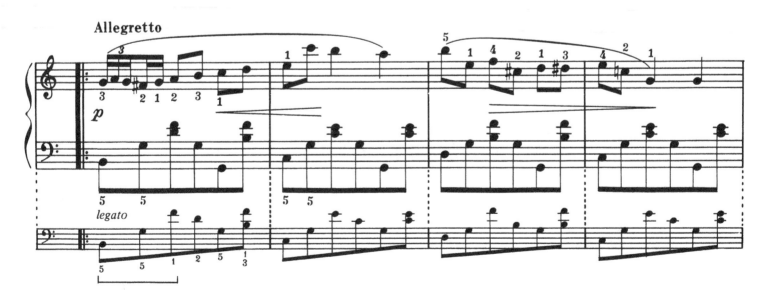

Looking Through An Old Album

from Youthful Days

Nikolai Rakov

Oriental Dance

Aram Khatchaturian
(1903 -   )

Chanson Triste

Vassili Kalinnikov
(1866 - 1901)

Simple Confession

Op. 20, No. 1

César Cui
(1835 - 1918)

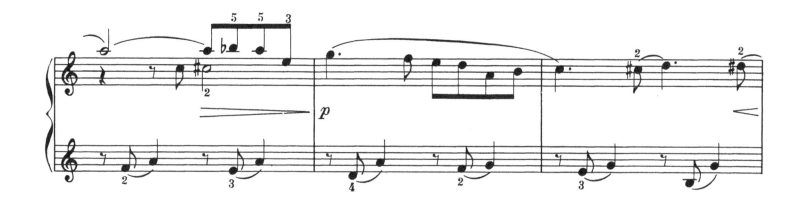

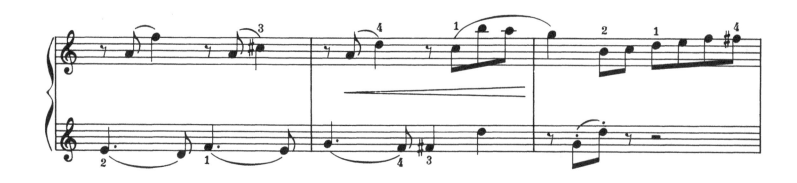

Evening

from Music for Children
Op. 65, No. 11

Serge Prokofiev
(1891 - 1953)

Andante teneroso

Rondo-March
Op. 60, No. 1

Dmitri Kabalevsky
(1904 -   )

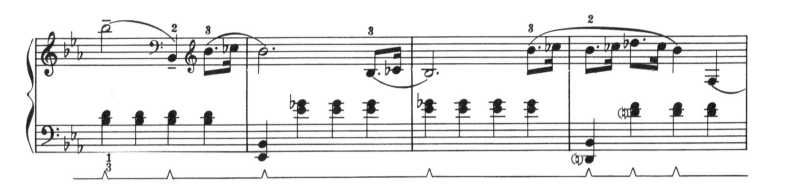

Prelude

Op. 34, No. 17

Dmitri Shostakovich
(1906 - 1975)

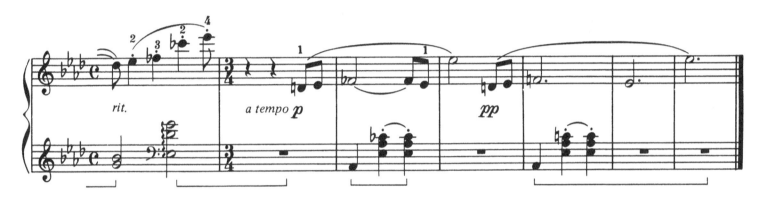

Prelude

Op. 37, No. 2

Alexander Gretchaninov
(1864 - 1956)

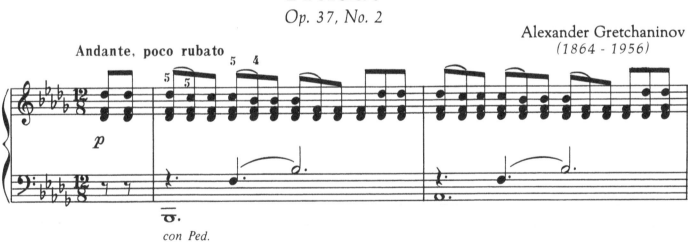

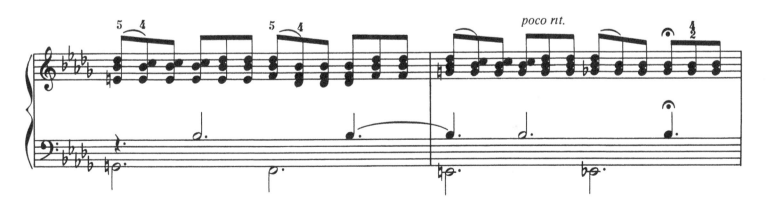

Romance

Op. 44, No. 1

Anton Rubinstein
(1829 - 1894)

The Hunter's Call

Fugetta Op. 43, No. 2

Nikolai Miaskovski
(1881 - 1950)

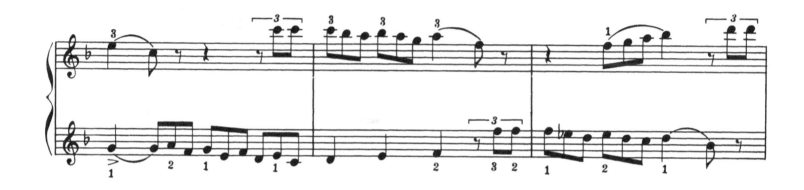

Prelude
Op. 38, No. 15

Dmitri Kabalevsky
(1904 -   )

Allegretto marcato

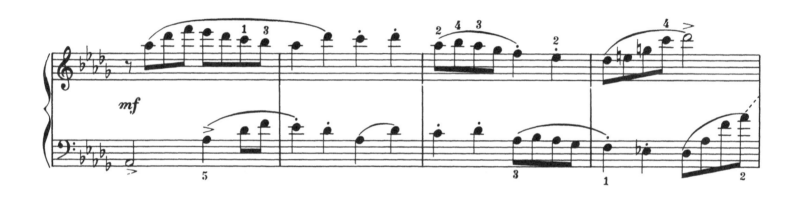

Polka Italienne

Serge Rachmaninoff
(1873 - 1943)

Originally written as a piano duet. The solo version most likely is either by the composer
or by Alexander Siloti to whom the work is dedicated.

(D.C. al Fine)

Autumn Song-October
Op. 37, No. 10

Peter I. Tchaikovsky
(1840 - 1893)

Andante doloroso e molto cantabile

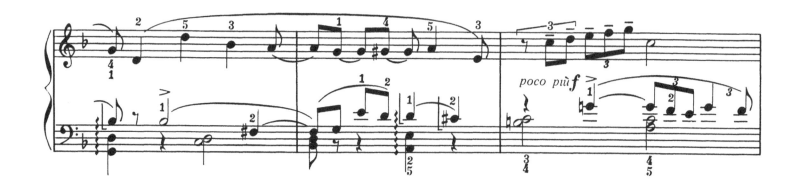

Reverie

Op. 25, No. 2

Anton Arensky
(1861 - 1906)

*Upper octaves may be omitted.

Prelude
Op. 31, No. 1

Reinhold Glière
(1875 - 1956)

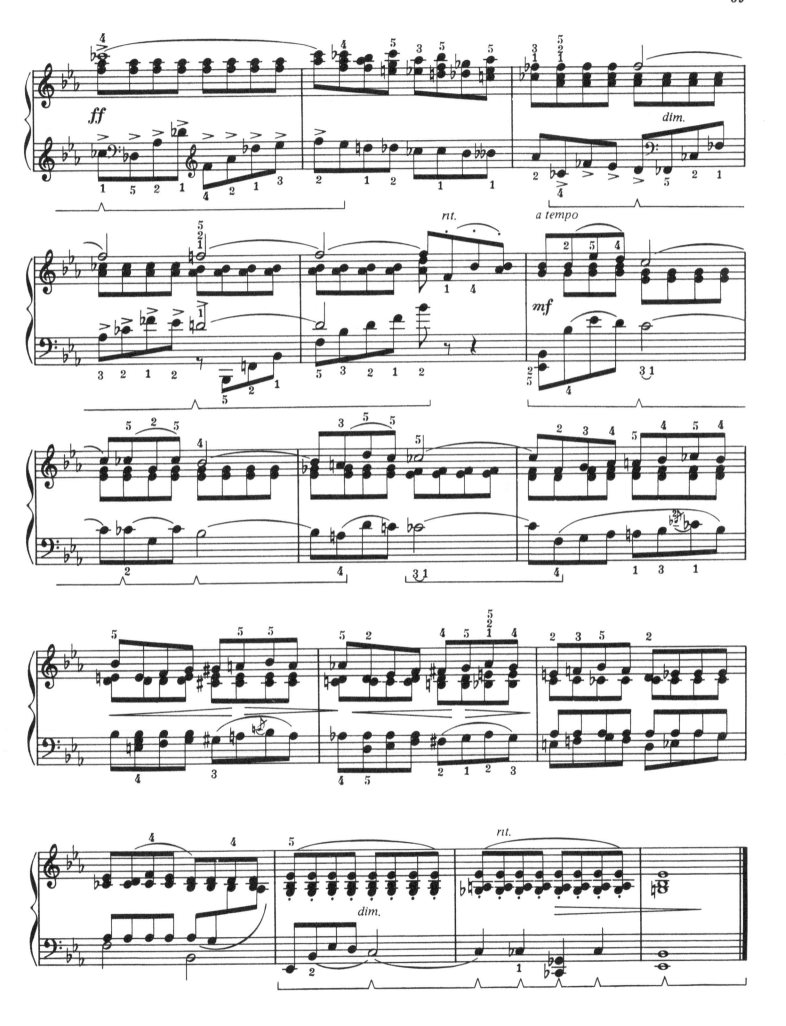

Nocturne
from Petite Suite

Alexander Borodin
(1833 - 1887)

Vision Fugitive
Op. 22, No. 3

Serge Prokofiev
(1891 - 1953)

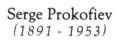

Allegretto

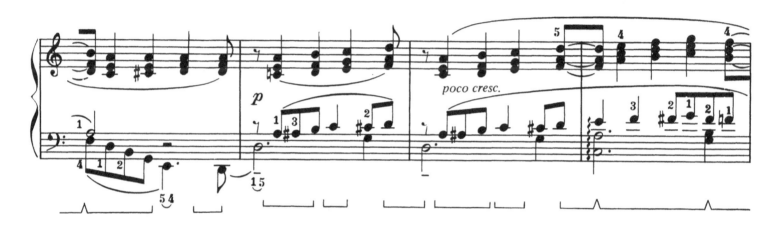

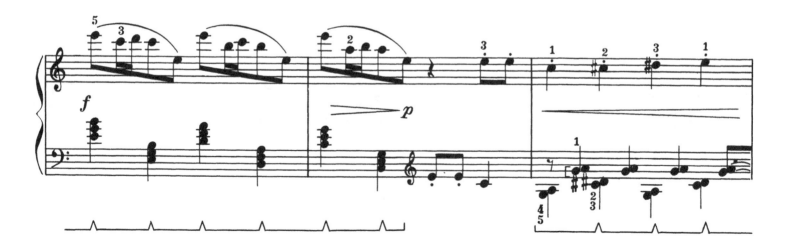

Album Leaf

Op. 45, No. 1

Alexander Scriabin
(1872 - 1915)

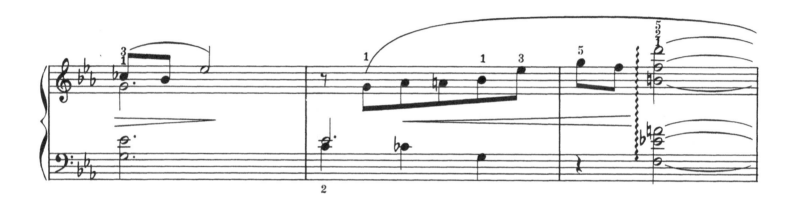

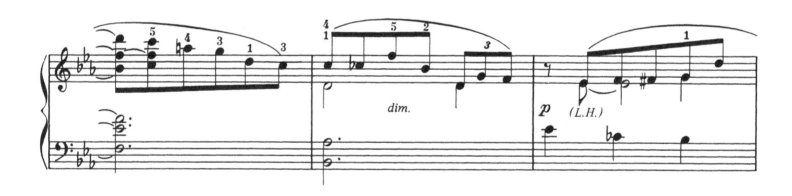

Bagatelle
Op. 5, No. 6

Alexander Tcherepnin
(1899 -   )

Allegro con spirito (♩= 100)

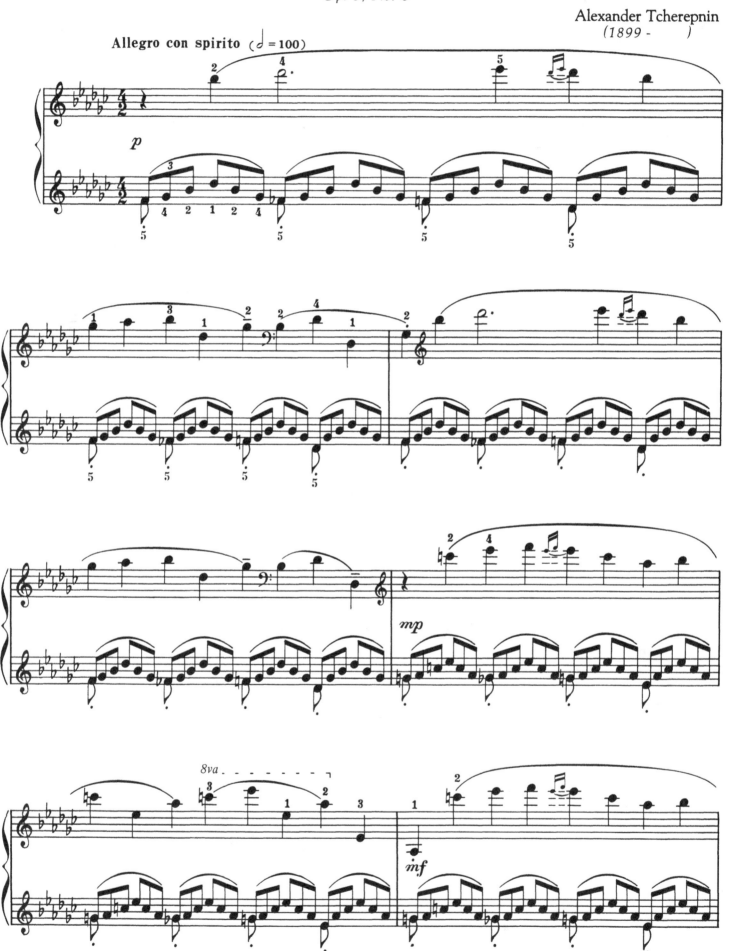

Promenade
from Pictures at an Exhibition

Modest Mussorgsky
(1839 - 1881)

Moderate commodo assai e con delicatezza

The Old Castle
from Pictures at an Exhibition

Modest Mussorgsky
(1839 - 1881)

Andante molto cantabile e con dolore

Mazurka

Mily Balakirev
(1837 - 1910)

Gavotte

from Classical Symphony, Op. 25

Serge Prokofiev
(1891 - 1953)

Arranged by the Composer

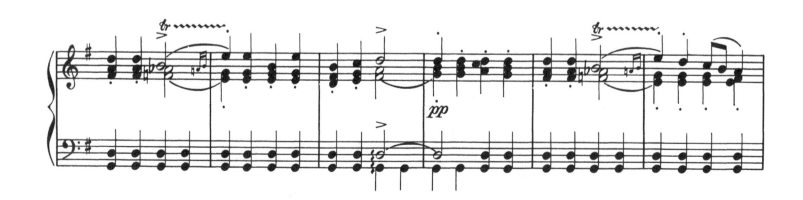

Prelude
Op. 11, No. 22

Alexander Scriabin
(1872 - 1915)

Dreaming

excerpt from Six Improvizations, Op. 74

Nikolái Miaskovsky
(1881 - 1950)

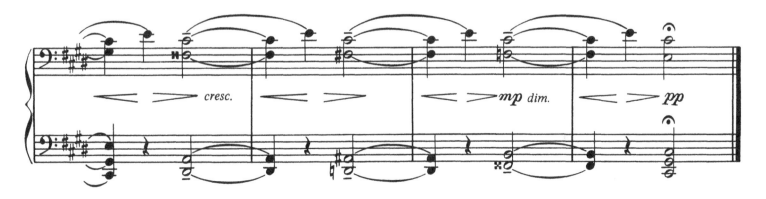

Romance

Op. 10, No. 6

Serge Rachmaninoff
(1873 - 1943)

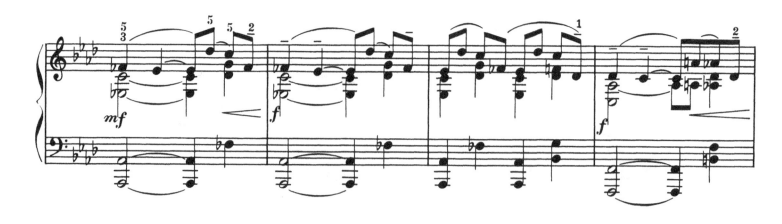

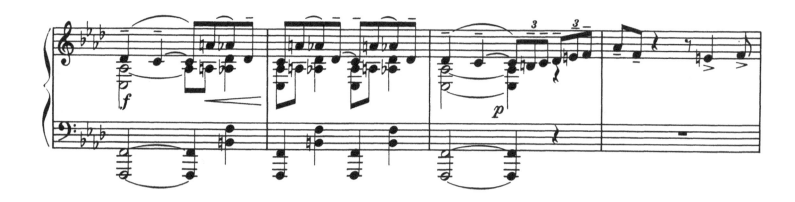